Happy Cooking
Gillian

INN FOOD

SEASONAL BREAKFASTS IN THE
WINE COUNTRY

RECIPES AND TEXT
GILLIAN KITE

PHOTOGRAPHY AND DESIGN
GAYE ALLEN

MEADOWLARK PUBLISHING

CALIFORNIA

contents

welcome to the Inn Food kitchen

The kitchen is the heart of the home and nowhere more so than at my Napa Valley Inns. I have been passionate about food and cooking for as long as I can remember. Whether watching my mother bake or put up preserves from the family garden, or feeling bewitched by the smells of a Polish dish created by my father from his own memories of his boyhood back on the farm, all of my warmest memories are of food and the kitchen.

Now, on their first morning staying at my Inn, my guests wake to the smells of breakfast cooking in the kitchen. The early risers come in for a chat and sip a cup of coffee as I bustle around preparing for the morning. We smile as we share the warmth of the kitchen.

My guests love my seasonal wine country breakfast, and I have been asked so many times for recipes that I knew I had to write this book. It is a culmination of all I have learned in over 30 years of cooking around the world; a celebration of the seasonal bounty in the Napa Valley; and most of all, an opportunity to share with you the warmth, love, friendship, and food of my kitchen.

With love,

Gillian

spring

bacon and onion scones

I must have picked up the habit of using leftovers in a creative way from my mother, who learned to be frugal in the austere Britain of the post-war years.

This recipe started with a few strips of crumbled cooked bacon, which made me wonder if a savory scone might be an interesting change from the sweet flavors one usually expects from this kind of pastry. Incorporating some green onions gives the recipe a welcome freshness to balance the cheese and bacon.

Preheat oven to 400°F.

Line a large baking sheet with parchment paper.

Sift the flour, baking powder, cream of tartar, salt, and pepper into a large mixing bowl. Add the rolled oats and combine.

Add the chopped green onions, diced ham, crumbled bacon, and the 2 cups grated cheese to the bowl. Mix together until the ingredients are evenly distributed.

In a small saucepan over medium heat, melt the ½ cup butter and let cool for a few minutes. In a small bowl, combine the melted butter with the milk and the mustard then add to the dough mixture, carefully mixing everything together with a spatula (do not overwork the dough). Turn the dough out onto a lightly floured work surface and divide into 2 even pieces. Form each piece into a 6-inch circle then cut each circle into 6 even wedges.

Place the 12 wedges on the prepared baking sheet. Melt the remaining 1 tablespoon butter, brush onto the wedges, and sprinkle with the remaining grated cheese.

Bake for 17 minutes. Cool on a wire rack.

MAKES 12 SCONES

2 cups all-purpose flour

1 tablespoon baking powder

1 teaspoon cream of tartar

1 teaspoon salt

1 teaspoon pepper

½ cup rolled oats

½ cup green onions, finely chopped

1 cup cooked diced ham

½ cup cooked crumbled bacon

2 cups grated cheese, plus 2 tablespoons

½ cup unsalted butter, plus 1 tablespoon

1 cup whole milk

1 tablespoon wholegrain mustard

GILL'S NOTES

This scone makes a good breakfast addition and can be made with any tasty, sharp cheese. I grew up less than 20 miles from the town of Cheddar, so you can guess my preference.

For a variation, cut the dough into small bite-size rounds with a pastry cutter (reduce the cooking time by a few minutes to accommodate) and serve the scone bites with an after-dinner cheese plate.

spinach and mushroom frittata

1 medium onion

3 tablespoons extra-virgin olive oil

½ large sweet red pepper

4 medium potatoes, cooked

1 cup small mushrooms

½ teaspoon paprika

8 cups baby spinach leaves

2 tablespoons chopped fresh oregano

Sea salt and freshly ground pepper

20 eggs

1 tablespoon water

3 cups grated cheese

1 tablespoon unsalted butter

GILL'S NOTES

This dish is great served warm with salsa, ideally a fresh pico de gallo (see recipe page 117) made with heirloom tomatoes from the garden. If you have leftovers, cut the frittata into little squares and serve with my tomato chutney (see recipe page 80) for a terrific appetizer.

Whether harvested from our plot in the community garden, the local farmers' market, or a friend's vegetable patch, I am lucky to get wonderful fresh produce throughout the year. Making a frittata is a versatile way to showcase the best of the season's bounty. Of course you can also add a breakfast meat, such as bacon or ham, as well. It's a very accommodating dish. This version, with baby spinach and mushrooms, is a favorite. If someone forages some springtime morels for you, this recipe would be a wonderful way to make use of them.

Preheat oven to 400°F.

Finely chop the onion and place in a medium sauté pan with 2 tablespoons of the olive oil. Gently fry over medium heat for 3–4 minutes. Finely chop the pepper and add to the onion. Peel the cooked potatoes and cut into ½-inch cubes. Slice the mushrooms. Add the potatoes, mushrooms, and paprika to the onion mixture. Continue to cook until the potatoes are slightly crispy. Add the spinach and 1 tablespoon of the chopped oregano and cook just until the spinach wilts, about 2–3 minutes. Season with salt and pepper. Set aside.

In a large bowl, mix together the eggs, water, and 2 cups of the cheese.

In a large ovenproof skillet (or paella pan) over medium-high heat, warm the remaining olive oil with the butter. When it begins to sizzle, add the egg mixture. Lower the heat and cook until the egg mixture begins to set on the outside but is still soft in the middle. Carefully add the cooked vegetables, spreading them evenly over the middle of the frittata. Sprinkle the remaining cheese and oregano over the top. Transfer to the oven and bake for 20 minutes.

SERVES 10

california cowboy breakfast

In England, Heinz Baked Beans are a staple that might be served with any meal of the day, from breakfast through supper. These are vegetarian beans rather than the more robust ham and barbecue sauce-laced varieties commonly found on American supermarket shelves. Searching for something tasty for my guests who don't eat meat, I was inspired by my baked-bean memories to turn out this more sophisticated version. We pair it with chicken apple sausage and poached eggs for a healthy and tasty modern-California version of a Western cowboy breakfast.

Preheat oven to 375°F.

Slice the onion, peel and crush the garlic, chop the olives and sundried tomatoes, and tear the basil into small pieces, setting aside half of the torn basil. Pour all but 2 tablespoons of the olive oil in the bottom of a large ovenproof dish with a lid. Drain and rinse the cannellini beans then place them in the baking dish along with the onions, garlic, olives, sundried tomatoes, tomato paste, and half of the basil. Season with salt and pepper. Gently toss until the ingredients are well mixed. Scatter the cherry tomatoes over the top and drizzle with the remaining olive oil. Cover and bake for 40 minutes.

Garnish with the reserved basil and serve.

SERVES 10

½ **large red onion**
2 **cloves garlic**
2 **tablespoons black olives**
2 **tablespoons sundried tomatoes**
2 **tablespoons fresh basil**
⅓ **cup lemon-infused olive oil**
2 **15-ounce cans cannellini beans**
2 **tablespoons tomato paste**
Salt and freshly ground black pepper
1 **cup cherry tomatoes**

GILL'S NOTES

I use local lemon-infused olive oil for these beans, but any decent extra-virgin olive oil will yield good results. This dish can be dressed up or down in numerous way for creative variations. I have used leftover puttanesca pasta sauce and sundried tomato bruschetta topping in place of the tomato paste and chopped olives. For a little heat, add a pinch of red pepper flakes. And for a non-vegetarian version, bake the sausage along with the beans.

I use a heavy cast-iron dish with a lid for this recipe. But if you don't have one, use your favorite casserole dish and simply cover it with a foil cap.

orange marmalade

The British climate is far too cold for any kind of citrus to grow outdoors. Despite this lack of local fruit, tangy orange marmalade is a breakfast staple served with toast and butter. With fresh juicy oranges now growing on my doorstep, I make this classic preserve every year.

5 medium oranges
4 cups sugar
Juice of 2 lemons

Preheat oven to 225°F.

Sterilize six 8-oz jars and their lids by cleaning them upside down in the dishwasher using the sanitizing cycle. Place the washed jars in the oven for about 30 minutes. Place a small saucer in the freezer.

Place the oranges in a large preserving pan, pour over enough water to cover, and bring to a boil. Gently boil for 1½–2 hours, making sure the oranges are covered with water the whole time. The oranges are ready when you can slide your knife into the skin easily and cannot see any white pith inside the skin.

Transfer the oranges to a large carving board with a grooved edge to catch the juices and leave for 15 minutes to cool. Rinse the preserving pan.

Once cool enough to handle, finely chop the oranges and return them to the pan with any of the juices on the cutting board. Add the sugar and lemon juice, and bring to a boil. Gently boil for 20 minutes or until setting point is reached. To check, place a small amount of the marmalade on the chilled saucer. If it wrinkles after a few minutes, the marmalade has set. Ladle the marmalade into the warm sterilized jars. Top with the lids and rings, sealing well.

MAKES SIX 8-OZ JARS

GILL'S NOTES

For a flavor variation, you can add 1 cup of crystallized ginger along with the sugar. Grapefruit can be substituted for the oranges.

breakfast bars

1 cup dates

½ cup fresh orange juice

2 cups raw almonds

1 cup dried apricots

½ teaspoon salt

½ cup raisins

½ cup raw pumpkin seeds

½ cup raw sunflower seeds

GILL'S NOTES

If you give the baking tin a quick spray of olive oil or other cooking spray before lining, the parchment paper will stick easily where you want it.

You can substitute different nuts and dried fruits for flavor variations. Just make sure to choose items with a similar consistency to the original ingredients to ensure the bars will hold together.

I always ask my guests if they have any dietary preferences or restrictions so I can adapt what I am cooking to their needs. A number of people require gluten-free food, so I thought I would try making a baked item without wheat flour for these guests to enjoy. The resulting bars are so tasty that all my guests wolf them down, not even knowing they are gluten free!

Preheat oven to 315°F.

Line a 13-by-9-inch shallow baking tin and a large baking sheet with parchment paper.

Pit and halve the dates and place in a bowl. Add the orange juice to cover and soak for 5 minutes.

Meanwhile, place the almonds and dried apricots in a food processor and pulse a few times until coarsely chopped. Add the salt, raisins, and dates with orange juice and pulse again until the mixture starts to stick together. Add the pumpkin seeds and sunflower seeds, pulsing a few more times to combine. Put the mixture into the prepared baking tin and press down carefully to form an even layer.

Bake for 40 minutes then cool for 30 minutes on a wire rack. Make 4 evenly spaced cuts lengthwise and crosswise to form 16 bars. Turn the baking tin upside down onto the prepared baking sheet. Gently separate the bars and space them out evenly, placing each bar cooked side down. Return to the oven and bake for 10 minutes. Cool before serving.

MAKES 16 BARS

maple oat scones

The scones I grew up with were delicate little treats. They were memorably served with clotted cream and strawberry jam accompanied by tiny crustless sandwiches as part of afternoon high tea, that now almost-extinct British tradition. With this background, I found American-style scones were not my cup of tea. Too dry and crispy for my liking and slathered with loads of oversweet frosting! One exception was when my eldest daughter Katie, working at Starbucks, brought home some maple oat scones for me to try. I liked them, and they soon became a favorite with my occasional latte. But I still found them on the dry side and began to think about making a scone that merged the best of both the British dainty and the American slugger. The secret turned out to be using cream of tartar, a standard in British recipes, instead of baking soda, and the result I think is a winner!

Preheat oven to 400°F.

Line a large baking sheet with parchment paper. Sift the flour, baking powder, cream of tartar, and salt into a large bowl. Add the chopped walnuts, brown sugar, and rolled oats. In a small saucepan over medium heat, melt the ½ cup butter and cool for a few moments. In a bowl, combine the melted butter, the maple syrup, ½ teaspoon of the maple extract, and the whipping cream and mix together. Add the butter mixture to the dry ingredients and gently combine with a spatula until a dough forms and starts to come away from the sides of the bowl.

Turn the dough out onto a lightly floured work surface and divide into 2 equal pieces. Form each piece into a 6-inch round then divide each round into 6 wedges. Place the 12 wedges on the prepared baking sheet and place a walnut half in the middle of each. Melt the remaining 1 tablespoon butter then brush on the tops of the scones. Sprinkle with the raw cane sugar. Bake for 15 minutes. Cool on a wire rack for 30 minutes.

To make the glaze, in a small bowl mix together the confectioners' sugar, the remaining ¼ teaspoon of maple extract, and warm water until the consistency is similar to thick liquid honey. Using a fork, drizzle the glaze over the scones. Allow the glaze to dry for a few minutes before serving.

MAKES 12 SCONES

2 cups all-purpose flour
1 tablespoon baking powder
1 teaspoon cream of tartar
¼ teaspoon salt
1 cup walnut pieces, chopped
⅓ cup light brown sugar
1 cup rolled oats
½ cup unsalted butter,
    plus 1 tablespoon
¼ cup maple syrup
¾ teaspoon maple extract
½ cup heavy whipping cream
12 walnut halves
1 tablespoon raw cane sugar
¾ cup confectioners' sugar

GILL'S NOTES

The only tricky part of this recipe is the glaze. You need just the right consistency to be able to drizzle fine zigzags over the scones. If you don't add enough liquid to the sugar, the resulting glaze will drop off your fork in oversweet globs; too much liquid and it will be transparent and sticky. When just right, the residual warmth from the scone will set up the glaze perfectly.

avocado and banana bread

¾ **cup unsalted butter**

¾ **cup light brown sugar**

1 **medium egg**

⅓ **cup canola oil**

1 **ripe banana**

2 **ripe avocados**

1 **teaspoon pure vanilla extract**

½ **cup pitted dates**

½ **cup pecan pieces**

2 **cups self-rising flour***

8 **pecan halves**

GILL'S NOTES

You can substitute many different nuts and fruits for this recipe; walnuts and cranberries are one great combination.

* If you cannot find self-rising flour, use 2 cups all-purpose flour mixed with 2 teaspoons baking powder and ½ teaspoon salt as a substitute.

California avocados are wonderful. One of my guests has a small avocado farm in the south of the state and brought me some beautiful specimens from her orchard. After making lots of savory dips and salads, I still had a few left over, creamy and delicious but just starting to darken at the edges.

I created this dish to use up the fruit and now I frequently leave a couple of avocados to become dark and fully ripe so I can make this savory bread.

Preheat oven to 350ºF.

Grease a 9-by-5-inch loaf pan and sprinkle with flour. Bring the butter to room temperature.

In the bowl of a stand mixer fiited with the whisk attachment, combine the ¾ cup of butter and the brown sugar until light and creamy. In a separate bowl, beat the egg and oil. Add the banana, avocados, and vanilla extract and mash together. Add to the butter mixture and mix on medium speed. Scrape down the sides of the bowl then mix for another minute.

Coarsely chop the dates and pecan pieces. Sift the flour into a mixing bowl and add the chopped pecans and dates.

Change the attachment on the stand mixer to the paddle attachment. Add the flour mixture and combine on slow speed for about 30 seconds until no dry flour is visible.

Pour the batter into the prepared loaf pan, smoothing the top with a knife. Arrange the pecan halves in a line along the top.

Bake for 1 hour and 20 minutes. Cool on a wire rack before turning out and slicing.

MAKES ONE 9-BY-5-INCH LOAF (10–12 SLICES)

english lemon curd

There is something wonderful about preserving the abundance of a harvest. I cannot pass by a tree burdened with fruit without asking its owner if I can gather some to transform into something delicious. In exchange, I usually offer several pots of a flavorful preserve. Whether you buy or grow your fruit, or even barter for it, this simple recipe is a great way to preserve the tart flavor of lemons.

Preheat oven to 225°F.

Sterilize six 8-oz jars with lids, a pitcher, and a sieve by cleaning them upside down in the dishwasher using the sanitizing cycle. Place the washed jars in the oven for 30 minutes.

In the top of a double boiler over low to medium heat, combine the egg yolks and sugar and whisk lightly. Stir in the lemon zest and juice. Cut the butter into cubes and add all at once. Melt slowly, stirring often, and cook the mixture until it is thick enough to coat the back of a wooden spoon, about 30 minutes.

Strain the curd through the fine-mesh sieve into the pitcher (this will make it easier to pour the curd into the jars). Divide the curd among the warm sterilized jars. Top with the lids, sealing well. Cool then refrigerate. For best results, enjoy within 1 month.

MAKES SIX 8-OZ JARS

6 egg yolks
1 cup sugar
Zest of 2 lemons
Juice of 6 lemons
½ cup unsalted butter

GILL'S NOTES

This curd is great with scones or hot buttered toast. And mixed with 1 cup of mascarpone, it makes a decadent filling for fruit tartlets.

You can use this same basic recipe to make a curd from virtually any citrus fruit: Meyer lemons, limes, or oranges. Adjust the amount of sugar according to the sweetness or tartness of the fruit. If you have lots of fruit, just scale up this recipe. Don't waste the egg whites; freeze them to use for meringues or heart-healthy omelets.

mum's easter biscuits

1½ cups unsalted butter

2 cups sugar, plus more for sprinkling

1 egg

6 drops of cassia oil

2¾ cups all-purpose flour

¼ cup currants

GILL'S NOTES

Cassia is the oil of cinnamon bark, and it adds a distinct and subtle flavor when used sparingly. You can find it at good health food stores.

Rolling the cookies between parchment paper stops the dough from sticking to the rolling pin without adding lots of flour, which makes the dough drier.

Baking sheets come in lots of different sizes; you can use whatever you have. It's ideal to use enough to ready all the cookies for baking at once. Whatever size you use, don't crowd the cookies or they will not bake evenly.

Easter in England is celebrated with chocolate eggs, hot cross buns and other unique delicacies. For me, it wouldn't be Easter without these delicious biscuits. The subtle taste of cinnamon from the cassia oil mixed with the creamy butter and the sweetness of the currants makes this one of my all-time favorite cookies.

Preheat oven to 350ºF.

Line four 16-by-12-inch baking sheets with parchment paper.

Bring the butter to room temperature. In the bowl of a stand mixer fitted with the whisk attachment, mix the butter and sugar for about 2 minutes until pale yellow. In a small bowl, beat together the egg and the cassia oil then add to the butter mixture. Pulse a few times to combine. Sift the flour into a bowl, then add to the butter and egg mixture. Add the currants. Change to the paddle attachment and mix together on slow speed until the ingredients form a dough.

Turn the dough out onto a lightly floured surface. Cut it into 4 equal parts and shape each part into a rough ball. Roll out each ball to a ¼-inch thickness between two pieces of parchment paper then cut out biscuits using a 3-inch diameter cookie cutter.

Place the rounds on the prepared baking sheets and bake for 15 minutes. Cool on a wire rack, then sprinkle with sugar.

MAKES 30

apricots with honey and orange

Fresh apricots are divine during their short season. Fortunately, even dried apricots capture some of that sweet sharp tang. When paired with spring oranges and honey, they create a dish that will wake up the taste buds. The enticing aroma of apricots and orange juice simmering on the stove in the morning will fill your kitchen with wonderful springtime scents.

Place the dried apricots and sparkling wine in a large sauté pan. Bring to a slow boil and cook until the liquid is reduced by half, about 3–4 mintues.

Reduce the heat to a simmer and add the orange juice, zest, and honey.

Simmer gently for 30–40 minutes, stirring occasionally with a wooden spoon, until the liquid is reduced to about 1 cup. Remove from the stove and cool.

Serve at room temperature with yogurt.

SERVES 6

3 cups dried apricots
1 cup sparkling white wine
3 cups fresh orange juice
Zest of 1 orange
⅓ cup honey
Yogurt for serving

GILL'S NOTES

I love the beautiful, thick, citrusy honey goodness covering these apricots. To vary the recipe, add ⅓ cup crystallized ginger at the same time as the orange zest for a spicy twist. You can also toast a few slivered almonds and sprinkle them over the apricots for a crunchy finish.

meyer lemonade

¼ cup water

½ cup sugar

7 Meyer lemons

2 cups ice cubes

8 cups sparkling water

GILL'S NOTES

Squeeze extra lemons when you make this recipe and then freeze the juice in an ice cube tray. You can use the juice in other recipes or add the frozen cubes to this lemonade or a lemon-lime soda for a stronger citrus flavor.

Meyer lemons are a cross between true lemons and mandarin oranges, giving them a slightly sweet flavor that's perfect for lemonade. They are easy to find in California, where they favor the climate. The tree is often grown as an ornamental; you might find you have one in your garden.

Spring in the Napa Valley is usually gorgeous, with warm sunny days and crisp nights, but it can vary from cool with showers to steaming hot. When we do get those Sahara-hot days, I make this refreshing drink to cool everyone down.

In a large saucepan over medium heat, warm the water and sugar until the sugar is dissolved, about 5 minutes. Set aside to cool.

Juice 6 of the lemons and cut the remaining lemon into fine slices. Add the lemon juice to the sugar syrup and pour into a large pitcher filled with ice. Add the lemon slices and top off with the sparkling water.

SERVES 8

summer

deep dish corn quiche

½ portion of mum's savory pastry
(see recipe page 118) or one
ready-made 9-inch pie crust

2 ears fresh corn on the cob

4 tablespoons extra-virgin olive oil

Sea salt and freshly ground black
pepper

½ yellow onion

½ red bell pepper

1 tablespoon fresh oregano

1 cup cooked diced ham

8 eggs

1½ cups heavy cream

2 cups grated cheese

GILL'S NOTES

*I usually use a medium Cheddar cheese
for this dish. You can substitute any
full-fat hard cheese, such as Emmental,
Gruyère, or Comté.*

*Here's an alternative to chopping the
fresh oregano, or any fresh herbs: rinse,
wrap in paper towel, and microwave for
1 minute. The leaves will be fragrant and
crumble away from the stems, ready to
add to your dish.*

Most quiches are flat and rather solid affairs, which is great if you want
something robust enough to slice and serve cold at a picnic. For breakfast fare,
I developed this more delicate version that puffs up like a soufflé.

Preheat oven to 400°F.

Roll out the pastry to form a 12-inch circle (or unwrap the pie crust if using). Gently place it
in an 8-inch fluted quiche pan. Freeze the pastry–lined pan for at least 30 minutes.

Husk the corn and brush the kernels with 2 tablespoons of the oil and season with salt and
pepper. Grill the corn, turning every few minutes, until the kernels are lightly roasted, about
10 minutes. Once cool, cut off the kernels and reserve.

Finely chop the onion, bell pepper, and oregano. Place each item, as well as the diced ham,
in a separate small bowl. In a large shallow frying pan over medium heat, warm the
remaining 2 tablespoons of oil. Add the onion and sauté until it starts to brown then add the
bell pepper and sauté until the pepper is softened, about 5 minutes. Add the ham,
corn, and oregano and continue to cook for a few more minutes. Remove from the heat
and cool for about 10 minutes.

In a bowl, beat together the eggs and heavy cream. Season with salt and pepper.

Place the chilled pastry–lined quiche pan on a baking sheet. Spread the corn mixture
evenly over the bottom. Cover with the grated cheese and then carefully pour over the
egg mixture. Bake for about 50 minutes, until the cheese melts and the top starts to
turn golden. Serve immediately.

SERVES 8

sweetcorn pancakes

The corn season here in Napa Valley is quite short. During the brief window, my friend Jeff the potter rides his bike to a big old house with a large garden where the one-time farmer helps his children grow heirloom sweet corn to sell for pocket money. When Jeff arrives, they pick it fresh for him and it must be eaten within a day before the natural sugars turn to starch. It is so sweet you could almost eat it straight from the cob! In this recipe, I use kernels from this super fresh corn, but frozen kernels or corn on the cob from the supermarket can be substituted.

Husk the corn and cut the kernels from the cobs, reserving half of the kernels in a large bowl. Place the remaining kernels in a food processor. Finely chop the cilantro, adding half to the bowl with the reserved kernels. Add the rest of the cilantro to the food processor. Coarsely chop the green onions and add to the food processor along with the eggs, flour, baking powder, salt, pepper, and paprika. Pulse for about 20 seconds to blend until a smooth consistency forms. Scrape the batter into the bowl with the reserved kernels and cilantro and mix thoroughly.

Grease a cast-iron skillet with the canola oil and warm over medium heat. Drop tablespoons of batter into the skillet and cook for 2–3 minutes. When small bubbles start to appear on the surface, use a spatula to flip the pancakes and cook on the other side for a few minutes more, until the top is golden brown. Test for doneness by carefully pushing a toothpick into the side of the pancake; if it comes out clean, the pancake is cooked. Serve immediately.

MAKES 20 PANCAKES

3 ears fresh corn on the cob
½ cup fresh cilantro
1 bunch green onions
3 large eggs
1 ½ cups all-purpose flour
1 tablespoon baking powder
½ teaspoon salt
½ teaspoon freshly ground black pepper
¼ teaspoon paprika
Canola oil for greasing

GILL'S NOTES

If using frozen corn, substitute 3 cups of kernels. Make sure you defrost the corn thoroughly before using. I like to serve these pancakes with a refreshing tomato, watermelon, and arugula salad or fresh pico de gallo (see recipe page 117).

blackberry clafoutis

4 cups fresh blackberries
½ cup ground almonds
2 tablespoons all-purpose flour
1 teaspoon baking powder
½ cup sugar
Zest of 1 lemon
4 medium eggs
1 ¼ cups heavy whipping cream

GILL'S NOTES

This is also yummy made with plums and substituting ground hazelnuts for the almonds. And if you have fresh cherries, try the traditional version. Just be careful of your teeth on those cherry pits!

Clafoutis is a traditional southern French dish with pancake-like batter. For purists, it can be made only with cherries, and cherries with the pits to boot because they add additional flavor. I love to use the summer blackberries that I pick from the hedgerows surrounding our friend's vineyards in place of the cherries. Strictly speaking, the French would call my version of this rich baked dish a flaugnarde and serve it for dessert. But I prefer calling it by its classic name and serving it for brunch.

Preheat oven to 325°F.

Grease a 10-inch round ovenproof dish and scatter the blackberries over the bottom. In a large bowl, combine the ground almonds, flour, baking powder, sugar, and lemon zest.

In another small bowl, whisk together the eggs and whipping cream. Add the egg mixture to the dry ingredients, mixing together until well combined. Carefully pour the batter over the blackberries.

Bake for about 35 minutes. Cool for 5 minutes and serve with vanilla yogurt (see recipe page 121).

SERVES 8

cherry and almond scones

Almond and cherry are flavors that work well together. Comprised of mostly pantry ingredients, you can make these scones any time of year. For a special treat, serve them with fresh juicy cherries in early summer.

Preheat oven to 400°F.

Line a large baking sheet with parchment paper. Sift the flour, cream of tartar, salt, and baking powder into a large mixing bowl. Add the ground almonds, brown sugar, dried cherries, and the 1 cup slivered almonds.

In a small saucepan over medium heat, melt the ½ cup butter and let cool for a few minutes. In a mixing bowl, combine the melted butter, cherry flavor, almond extract, and whipping cream. Pour the butter mixture into the flour mixture and carefully fold together until a dough forms and comes away from the sides of the bowl.

Turn the dough out onto a lightly floured work surface. Divide the dough into half and gently shape each half into a 6-inch round. Cut each round into 6 wedges. Place the 12 scones on the prepared baking sheet.

Melt the remaining 1 tablespoon butter and brush over the scones. Sprinkle with the remaining 2 tablespoons almonds and the cane sugar.

Bake for 15 minutes.

MAKES 12 SCONES

2 cups all-purpose flour
1 teaspoon cream of tartar
¼ teaspoon salt
1 tablespoon baking powder
½ cup ground almonds
⅓ cup light brown sugar
1 cup dried cherries
1 cup slivered blanched almonds,
plus 2 tablespoons
½ cup unsalted butter, plus
**   1 tablespoon**
½ teaspoon natural cherry flavoring
½ teaspoon almond extract
1 cup heavy whipping cream
1 tablespoon raw cane sugar

GILL'S NOTES

It can be hard to find natural cherry flavoring or extract. Raspberry extract, available in most supermarkets, can be used instead.

Over-kneading the dough will yield tough scones; handle it gently and you'll be rewarded with a light and fluffy texture that melts in your mouth.

apricot and walnut cookies

1 ½ cups unsalted butter

1 ¾ cups white sugar

Zest of 1 large orange

3 cups all-purpose flour

1 tablespoon baking powder

1 cup medium ground cornmeal

½ teaspoon salt

4 egg yolks

1 teaspoon pure vanilla extract

1 cup dried apricots, chopped

1 cup walnuts, chopped

GILL'S NOTES

If you like your cookies less crunchy, use a finer grade of corn meal or substitute with semolina flour.

I have fond memories of the longest vacation of my life, a whole month spent on the beautiful island of Corsica. This rugged, mountainous island is most famous for producing sweet chestnuts, but I recall the beautiful apricots and sweet clementines that inspired me to make these cookies. When I bite into the crunch of the corn and the walnuts and taste the fresh orange tang with the sweetness of the apricots, I can just close my eyes and imagine drinking my early morning coffee looking out at the clear blue Mediterranean Sea.

Preheat oven to 300°F.

Line a few cookie sheets with parchment paper. Bring the butter to room temperature.

In the bowl of a stand mixer fitted with the paddle attachment, combine the butter, 1 ½ cups of the sugar, and the orange zest and beat for about 1 minute until creamy and pale yellow.

Sift the flour and baking powder into a medium bowl. Add the cornmeal and salt and set aside. In a small bowl, whisk together the egg yolks and vanilla extract and add to the butter mixture. Blend on medium speed for a few seconds until evenly mixed. Add the flour mixture and combine on low speed for a few seconds. Add the chopped apricots and walnuts, scrape down the sides of the bowl, and pulse several times until the dough forms into a ball.

Place the remaining ¼ cup of sugar in a shallow dish.

Turn the dough out onto a lightly floured work surface and divide it into 32 equally sized pieces. Form each piece into a smooth ball then roll each ball in the sugar until evenly coated. Press lightly on the sugared balls with the palm of your hand to make a circular disc about 3 ½ inches in diameter. Place 1 inch apart on the prepared cookie sheets.

Bake on the center rack of the oven for 12–15 minutes, until the cookies just start to brown at the edges.

MAKES 32 COOKIES

banana and honey bread

One of the joys of owning an inn is meeting fellow foodies and travelers. One delightful couple has beehives and they always bring me a jar of their delicious honey whenever they visit. I use their honey to make this recipe, (if I haven't already eaten it up by the spoonful beforehand!).

Preheat oven to 350ºF.

Grease and flour a 9-by-5-inch loaf pan. Sift the flour into a large bowl, then add the freshly grated nutmeg. Bring the butter to room temperature. In the bowl of a stand mixer fitted with the paddle attachment, combine the butter, sugar, and lemon zest until the mixture is an even pale yellow, about 2 minutes.

In a bowl, mash the bananas and mix well with the eggs, lemon extract, and 4 tablespoons of the honey. Add to the butter mixture, then add the sifted flour and nutmeg. Combine for about 1 minute until evenly blended.

Pour the batter into the prepared loaf pan and bake for 1 hour until a skewer comes out clean. Cool on a wire rack for 5 minutes.

Warm the remaining 1 tablespoon honey in a small saucepan and brush over the warm bread. Let cool completely before slicing and serving.

MAKES ONE 9-BY-5-INCH LOAF (10–12 SLICES)

1 ½ cups self-rising flour*
¼ teaspoon freshly grated nutmeg
½ cup unsalted butter
½ cup sugar
Zest of 1 lemon
2 ripe bananas
2 medium eggs
½ teaspoon lemon extract
5 tablespoons honey

GILL'S NOTES

This light bread is great when you want to serve something for people that have nut allergies. It is delicious on its own or served with butter and a homemade preserve; blackberry is my favorite. You can also serve it with whipped honey butter: just take a tablespoon of honey and whip it into four tablespoons of softened butter.

* If you cannot find self-rising flour, use 1 ½ cups of all-purpose flour mixed with 1 ½ teaspoons of baking powder and ¼ teaspoon of salt as a substitute.

green fig preserve

6 cups fresh green figs

4 cups sugar

2 lemons

½ cup water

GILL'S NOTES

This is an easy recipe but be careful not to let the figs boil too vigorously or you'll end up with a fig mush instead of nice fig pieces. The sugar is warmed before adding for the same reason: to avoid too much boiling and loss of texture in the figs.

An alternative to the cold-plate wrinkle test for setting point is to observe the cooling jam on your wooden spoon. If it is at set point, it will form a small drop or flake on the edge of the spoon. This takes a little more experience than the plate method but is quicker once you get the idea. Try it alongside the plate test to see how it looks. Of course, if you have a jam thermometer you can simply measure the setting point at 220°F.

Figs are amazing things. A minute wasp pollinates every one. Too much pollination and the fig will grow so big it will split right open. The tree itself can be so prolific it will break itself. Our friends at a local winery were awoken one night by a crack like lightning, but on a cloudless summer night. When they investigated they found their old fig tree had split in two under the weight of the beautiful green figs. I now make it my mission to save every tree I can by collecting these lovely figs and preserving them with this recipe!

Preheat oven to 225°F.

Sterilize six 8-oz jars and their lids by cleaning them upside down in the dishwasher using the sanitizing cycle. Place the washed jars in the oven for about 30 minutes. Place a small saucer in the freezer to use for testing the setting point.

Spread the sugar out on a baking sheet then place in the oven for about 30 minutes.

Remove the stems from the figs and cut them lengthwise into quarters. In a large heavy-bottomed pot, combine the figs, the lemon juice and zest, and the water. Bring to a simmer over low heat and cook until the figs are soft, about 10 minutes. Add the warmed sugar and bring to a gentle boil. Continue to heat, stirring constantly, until the mixture starts to thicken. To test if the preserve has reached setting point, place 1 teaspoon onto the chilled saucer. Let it sit for about 1 minute then gently push the cooled mixture. If set, a distinct wrinkle will be visible on the top of the jam.

Ladle the warm fig preserve into the sterilized jars and seal with the lids.

MAKES SIX 8-OZ JARS

breakfast jam

6 cups mixed fruit (see note below)
Juice and zest of 2 lemons
⅓ cup water
4 cups sugar

GILL'S NOTES

Some fruits, if not overripe, have natural pectin, which you need for the jam to set. As long as you combine fruit from each of the following two groups you should get a good set without adding pectin.

Group 1: apples, blackberries, citrus zest, currants, gooseberries, plums, raspberries

Group 2: apricots, blueberries, cherries, figs, peaches, pears, pineapples, strawberries

If your balance is not quite right and your jam is not setting, add some extra apples or citrus zest.

.

Seasonal fruits, both fresh and cooked, are always a part of breakfast that my Inn guests really enjoy. However, as I find it hard to say no to the wonderful produce at the local farm stands and farmer's markets, I often find I have bought more than my guests can consume. Since I hate to see anything go to waste I thought of this jam as a great way to make good use of my extra fruit.

Preheat oven to 225°F.

Sterilize six 8-oz jars and their lids by cleaning them upside down in the dishwasher using the sanitizing cycle. Place the washed jars in the oven for about 30 minutes. Place a small saucer in the freezer to use for testing the setting point.

In a large heavy-bottomed pot, combine the fruit, lemon juice and zest, and water. Bring to a simmer over low heat and cook until the fruit softens, about 10 minutes. Add the sugar and gently boil for 30–40 minutes. To test if the preserve has reached setting point, place 1 teaspoon onto the chilled saucer. If the surface wrinkles after 1–2 minutes, the jam has set.

Ladle the jam into warm sterilized jars, seal with the lids, and cool well before serving.

MAKES SIX 8-OZ JARS

blueberry coconut muffins

Everybody loves a light and fluffy muffin, and blueberry muffins are an American classic. I like the flavor of blueberries alone; with the added twist of texture and flavor from shredded coconut and coconut milk they are even better. As a bonus, these muffins often work for my guests with tree nut allergies, as many people can still eat coconut.

Preheat oven to 400°F.

Grease a standard 12-count muffin tin or line with standard paper muffin cups.

Sift the flour into a large bowl. Add the sugar, shredded coconut, blueberries and Meyer lemon zest and gently mix until the ingredients are evenly distributed. In a medium saucepan over medium heat, melt the butter and let cool for a few minutes. Add the coconut milk and egg to the melted butter and mix together. Pour into the flour mixture and carefully fold together, making sure not to break the blueberries. Divide the batter among the 12 muffin cups.

Bake for 24 minutes. The muffins will be ready when a toothpick inserted in the center of a muffin comes out clean.

MAKES 12 MUFFINS

2 cups self-rising flour *
½ cup sugar
1 cup shredded coconut
1 cup blueberries
Zest of 1 Meyer lemon
½ cup unsalted butter
1 14-oz can coconut milk
1 large egg

GILL'S NOTES

As an alternative, I like to use a cup of the first, slightly firm summer strawberries, chopped into about half-inch dice, and the zest of an orange. Top each muffin with a blackberry.

* If you cannot find self-rising flour, use 2 cups all-purpose flour mixed with 2 teaspoons baking powder and ½ teaspoon salt as a substitute.

damper

4 cups all-purpose flour

2 tablespoons baking powder

1 tablespoon baking soda

1 tablespoon sugar

1 teaspoon salt

4 tablespoons unsalted butter

1 cup water

½ cup whole milk, plus 1 tablespoon

GILL'S NOTES

This bread is great for breakfast with butter and your favorite homemade preserve. You can also serve it alongside a nice soup, or use leftovers for a panzanella salad with some lovely heirloom tomatoes.

Imagine a rugged Aussie in the Outback, a Crocodile Dundee-type, if you are old enough to remember that character. As the sun goes down he whips together a rough bread, bakes it in the ashes of his fire, and enjoys it with golden syrup. In Australia tales of these damper breads are the stuff of legend, and avid campers still make them today as an act of homage to their swagmen and drover forebears. This quick recipe for a free-form, no-yeast soda bread will give you the fulfillment of a hearty loaf without having to battle crocs, roos, or other dangers of the bush!

Preheat oven to 400°F.

Line a medium baking sheet with parchment paper. Sift the flour, baking powder, baking soda, sugar, and salt into a large mixing bowl.

In a medium saucepan over medium heat, melt the butter and cool for a few minutes. Add the water and milk to the melted butter and mix thoroughly. Make a well in the middle of the flour mixture. Gently pour in the butter mixture, bringing the dough together from the sides of the bowl. Turn out onto a lightly floured work surface and knead just until smooth.

Shape the dough into an 8-inch round and place on the prepared baking sheet. Using a knife, make a ½-inch deep by 3-inch long cross in the center. Brush with the 1 tablespoon milk and sprinkle with flour.

Bake for 45 minutes or until the bread feels hollow when tapped on the bottom. Cool for 10 minutes before serving.

MAKES ONE 8-INCH ROUND LOAF (8-10 SLICES)

bergamot iced tea

In England I would never drink a cold, much less iced, cup of tea. After all these years living in American, I still need a cup of hot Earl Grey tea to wake me up and start the day. As you can imagine, it has taken me a while to get my head around the idea of a cold cuppa. That said, the glorious climate of the Napa Valley is rather different than the weather where I am from. So I decided I had to merge a bit of my heritage, with a bergamot and blackcurrant twist, to make an iced tea even a skeptic like me can enjoy on a hot summer's day.

Place the teabags in a teapot and add the boiling water. Leave for at least 1 hour to allow the flavors to steep. Remove the teabags. Cut the lemon in $1/8$-inch slices. Fill a large glass pitcher half full with ice and some of the lemon slices. Pour in the tea and mix with a wooden spoon.

Fill 4 glasses with ice. Top with the iced tea and a splash of blackcurrant cordial. If you like your tea sweeter, add some raw cane sugar or honey to taste. Add lemon slices and serve.

SERVES 4

2 Earl Grey tea bags
1 lemon
4 cups boiling water
½ cup blackcurrant cordial
Raw cane sugar or honey

GILL'S NOTES

You can freeze some of the mix in your ice tray to make iced-tea cubes for those hot sunny days when you want to finish off your chilled glass without diluting the flavor. You can also freeze just the diluted blackcurrant cordial with some lemon juice and add these dark cubes to the iced tea for a visual and taste contrast.

fall

baked cinnamon apple pancake

Two American breakfast classics are pancakes and cinnamon rolls. A typical stack of pancakes is usually served with lashings of syrup, butter, fruit or cream, whereas the cinnamon roll already has its own sweet and gooey filling and needs no additions. Inspired by these two dishes, wonderful fall apples, and memories of my dad frying apples in butter, I created this recipe for a baked pancake as a celebration of American flavors in an old-school European style.

Preheat oven to 375°F.

Peel, core, and cut the apples into ½-inch slices. Place the slices in a bowl with the lemon juice (this will help keep the apples from turning brown). Set aside.

Sift the flour, baking powder, salt, and ½ cup of the sugar into a medium bowl. In a small bowl, mix together the remaining ¼ cup sugar with the 1 teaspoon of ground cinnamon. In a large bowl, mix together the whipping cream, eggs, and vanilla extract. Add the egg mixture to the flour mixture and whisk until thoroughly combined.

Melt the butter in a 14-inch ovenproof skillet over medium-high heat. Add the apple slices and sauté for 5 minutes until they turn light golden brown but are still slightly firm. Add the cinnamon sugar and cook for 1 minute. Lower the heat to medium then pour in the batter, making sure to cover the apple slices. Cook until the edges of the pancake start to brown, about 5 minutes. Carefully place the pan in the oven for about 20 minutes and bake until the top of the pancake turns an even brown and has risen slightly. Serve with confectioners' sugar and maple syrup.

SERVES 8

4 large apples
Juice of 1 lemon
¾ cup all-purpose flour
1 tablespoon baking powder
½ teaspoon salt
¾ cup sugar
1 teaspoon ground cinnamon
1 cup heavy whipping cream
10 large eggs
1 teaspoon pure vanilla extract
4 tablespoons unsalted butter
1 teaspoon confectioners' sugar
Maple syrup

GILL'S NOTES

This cousin of a Dutch or German apple pancake will puff up a bit during baking because of the eggs in the batter. You can substitute firm pears for the apples in this recipe.

breakfast tomatoes

12 medium tomatoes

2 tablespoons extra-virgin olive oil

1 tablespoon balsamic vinegar

8 leaves fresh basil, torn

1 teaspoon freshly ground sea salt

½ teaspoon freshly ground white pepper

GILL'S NOTES

Use the best, ripest tomatoes you can find for this recipe. If buying from your local store, Campari are one of the most flavorful commercial varieties. If your tomatoes are not perfectly ripe, drizzle them with agave nectar before cooking to add a hint of sweetness to the dish.

The abundance of wonderful tomatoes is one of the delights of summer. Tomato vines seem to like the Napa Valley as much as grape vines do. My friend Barney Welsh, at Forni Brown Welsh gardens, knows that he can always rely on me to take the "splitters." These are late-season tomatoes that are super ripe and have burst their skins. They taste wonderful, but for the French Laundry and Barney's other exclusive restaurant customers, they have to look perfect as well. Which means more for me to use making chutneys, pasta sauces, fresh salsas, or these baked tomatoes to serve with one of my deep-dish quiches for breakfast.

Preheat oven to 375°F.

Place each tomato on its side and slice in half. Arrange the 24 tomato halves skin side down in a 12-by-9-inch baking dish. Drizzle with the olive oil and vinegar. Scatter the torn basil leaves over the tomatoes and season with the salt and pepper.

Bake for 40 minutes and serve immediately.

SERVES 6

sausage and sweet red pepper plait

Sausage rolls are a British cousin of pigs in a blanket, though made with bangers rather than hot dogs. My mum made a more refined version, which she flattened, topped with tomato sauce, and sliced for tea. My own take for breakfast features individual portions that look good and are easy to serve.

Preheat oven to 400ºF. Line a large baking sheet with parchment paper.

Finely chop the onion, pepper, and oregano. In a medium frying pan over medium heat, warm the olive oil. Add the onions, peppers, oregano, and paprika and genty fry until softened but not browned. Season with salt and pepper, transfer to a bowl, and set aside.

Lightly flour a pastry board or cool work surface. Divide the pastry in half and roll each portion out into a 12-by-8-inch rectangle. Cut each rectangle into four smaller rectangles, each 3-by-8-inches. You will have 8 pieces of pastry.

Divide the sausage meat (if using links, remove the skins) among the 8 pieces, placing the sausage in the middle of each and flattening it out to cover the center of the pastry to the edges. Place 1 teaspoon of the onion mixture on top of the sausage. Cut the tomato into 8 thin slices and place 1 slice, along with a basil leaf, on top. Each piece should have only the middle third of pastry covered with toppings.

Using a sharp knife, make 3 evenly spaced cuts in the pastry on either side of the sausage mixture. Be sure to cut all the way to the uncovered edges so that each side of the sausage has 4 pastry ribbons that are still attached. Braid (or "plait" as we would say) the pastry ribbons over the top of the sausage to make a neat parcel. Carefully place the parcels on the prepared baking sheet. Mix the egg yolk with the heavy cream and brush over the top of the braided parcels. Bake for 30 minutes. Serve hot with scrambled eggs or cold with piccalilli (see recipe page 78).

SERVES 8

½ **medium sweet onion**
1 **large red pepper**
1 **teaspoon fresh oregano**
1 **tablespoon extra-virgin olive oil**
¼ **teaspoon paprika**
Sea salt and freshly ground pepper
1 **lb. cream cheese pastry,**
   (see recipe page 118)
1 **lb. good New York breakfast**
   sausage, or eight 2-oz links
1 **large beefsteak tomato**
8 **small fresh basil leaves**
1 **egg yolk**
2 **tablespoons heavy cream**

GILL'S NOTES

If you don't have time to make and roll out homemade pastry, you can substitute with store-bought frozen puff pastry, which comes 2 sheets to a package. Follow the package directions for defrosting before use. If you make extra pepper mixture, it will keep in the refrigerator for 1 week in a covered container.

For a rich and tasty vegetarian version, use mushrooms in place of the sausage. Season a few sliced mushrooms with salt and pepper then saute them with fresh herbs in equal parts butter and olive oil.

chardonnay baked pears with honey

3 medium Comice pears

2 tablespoons honey

½ cup chardonnay

1 tablespoon raw cane sugar

GILL'S NOTES

Chardonnay is my choice of wine for this dish; I definitely prefer a Burgundy-style wine with no or little oak aging. You can substitute any decent fruity white wine. This dish is also a great way to use up leftover Champagne that has lost its fizz.

To make easy work of drizzling honey, first transfer it to a plastic squeeze bottle with a small tip

If I had to choose one dish that sums up my cooking style, this might be it. Quick and easy to prepare, it's made from a few simple ingredients yet is impressive to look at and has great seasonal flavors.

Much of the Napa Valley was orchards and nut groves before grapes and wine became king. In the surrounding counties, wonderful pears are still grown in profusion. We have a long pear season that starts with Bartletts in late summer, progresses through Bosc and Comice in the fall, and ends with the winter Anjou. Any of these pears work well in this dish, but my favorite is the smooth sweet Comice paired with an unoaked Chardonnay.

Preheat oven to 375°F.

Halve and core the pears. Cut each half into fine slices from stem to base. Arrange the pear slices evenly in a 10-inch baking dish, pushing and fanning them out so they lie flat in the dish. Drizzle the honey over on top, then pour over the wine, and sprinkle with the raw cane sugar.

Bake for 45 minutes then cool for 10 minutes. Serve for breakfast with homemade yogurt (see recipe page 121), or as a dessert with crème fraiche.

SERVES 6

pumpkin pie scones

Pumpkins start to appear around here at the beginning of October, when giants are harvested and sometimes displayed at local wineries or grocery stores. Moving through the month, smaller carved and candled versions appear as Halloween approaches. Then, with Thanksgiving in November and traditional pumpkin pie, we finally get to eat them! Not wanting to wait that long, I decided to make these light and fluffy scones to give my guests a pumpkin treat throughout the fall.

Preheat oven to 400°F.

Line a large baking sheet with parchment paper.

Sift the flour, baking powder, cream of tartar, salt and pumpkin pie spice into a large mixing bowl. Chop the pecans and add them to the flour mixture along with the brown sugar, rolled oats, and cranberries.

In a small saucepan over medium heat, melt the ½ cup of butter then cool for a few minutes. Once cooled, pour the melted butter into another bowl and mix together with the pureed pumpkin and cream. Carefully combine with the dry ingredients to form a soft dough.

Turn the dough out onto a lightly floured work surface and divide into 2 equal pieces. Shape each piece into a 6-inch round then cut each round into 6 wedges. Place the 12 wedges on the prepared baking sheet.

Melt the remaining 1 tablespoon butter, brush it over the scones, then sprinkle with the pumpkin seeds and raw cane sugar. Bake for 15 minutes. Cool on a wire rack and serve.

MAKES 12 SCONES

---

2 cups all-purpose flour
1 tablespoon baking powder
1 teaspoon cream of tartar
¼ teaspoon salt
1 teaspoon pumpkin pie spice
1 cup pecans
½ cup light brown sugar
½ cup rolled oats
1 cup dried cranberries
½ cup unsalted butter,
    plus 1 tablespoon
½ cup cooked pureed pumpkin,
½ cup heavy whipping cream
1 tablespoon pumpkin seeds
1 tablespoon raw cane sugar

GILL'S NOTES

Pumpkins come in lots of varieties; best for pies are the smaller, sweeter sugar pumpkins. You can recycle your unused Halloween pumpkins, but they will have a stringier texture and will need a little more sugar. Cook your own pumpkin by steaming deseeded slices for about 30 minutes, or place the same pieces skin side down on a baking sheet and bake at 350°F for about 45 minutes. With either method, puree the cooked pumpkin before using. Canned pumpkin works well, too.

zucchini spice bread

2 cups self-rising flour*

¾ cup light brown sugar

1 teaspoon ground cinnamon

½ teaspoon ground ginger

¼ teaspoon ground nutmeg

½ teaspoon salt

1 cup rolled oats

3 large eggs

¾ cup canola oil

½ teaspoon pure vanilla extract

2 medium zucchini

1 tablespoon brown cane sugar

GILL'S NOTES

This moist, spicy bread keeps well for a couple of days if stored in an airtight container. Enjoy on its own or with butter or baked fruit and yogurt.

* If you cannot find self-rising flour, use 2 cups all-purpose flour mixed with 2 teaspoons baking powder and ½ teaspoon salt as a substitute.

In the British climate of my youth, my dad needed a heated greenhouse to grow tomatoes, cucumbers, melons, or zucchini. Here in the Napa Valley, they all grow like weeds. In my husband Nick's plot at the community garden, he usually finds room between the rows of heirloom tomatoes to plant a couple of zucchini varieties.

The plants just explode and end up covering most of the garden. The fruits are so prolific they need to be picked almost daily; left even for a couple of days they can grow to the size of vegetable marrows. I created this delicious spiced bread to use up some of this bounty.

Preheat oven to 350ºF.

Grease a 9-by-5-inch loaf pan and dust with flour. Sift the flour, sugar, cinnamon, ginger, nutmeg, and salt into a large bowl and then add the rolled oats. In a small bowl, whisk together the eggs, canola oil, and vanilla extract. Coarsely grate the zucchini on a box grater. Make a well in the middle of the dry ingredients, add the grated zucchini and egg mixture, and mix together until just combined.

Pour the batter into the prepared loaf pan, smoothing the top with a knife. Sprinkle with the cane sugar. Bake for 1 hour then let cool completely on a wire rack before turning out and slicing.

MAKES ONE 9-BY-5-INCH LOAF (10–12 SLICES)

piccalilli

4 small zucchini

1 medium cauliflower

1 lb. French beans

1 lb. white pearl onions

1 cucumber

1 tablespoon salt

1-inch piece ginger root

½ cup all-purpose flour

½ cup English mustard powder

3 tablespoons turmeric

¼ teaspoon freshly grated nutmeg

2 ½ cups white distilled vinegar

1 ⅓ cup sugar

GILL'S NOTES

This rich crunchy pickle makes a pleasant accompaniment to any kind of egg, cheese, or cold meat dish. The acid is a great counterpoint when served with a frittata or quiche for breakfast.

For a classic ploughman's lunch, serve this with a hunk of great British Cheddar cheese and a crusty roll.

My dad was of solid Polish peasant stock and was never happier than when puttering in his garden and producing mountains of glorious fruits and vegetables. Mum would dutifully can, preserve, pickle, freeze and otherwise make use of the bounty so that we could savor it long beyond harvest.

With two bed-and-breakfast inns and a couple of dozen people for breakfast every morning, I have a ready outlet for most of what my husband Nick produces from his vegetable garden. Even so, there are times when the combination of the incredible Napa Valley climate and Nick's gardening skills produces more zucchini, cucumbers, and green beans than anyone can reasonably consume. On these occasions I make this traditional British piccalilli.

Preheat oven to 225°F.

Sterilize six 8-oz jars and their lids by cleaning them upside down in the dishwasher using the sanitizing cycle. Place the washed jars in the oven for about 30 minutes.

Cut the zucchini into dice, and break the cauliflower into small florets. Trim and half the French beans. Peel the pearl onions. Deseed the cucumber and cut into dice. Place the prepared vegetables in a large mixing bowl. Sprinkle with salt, cover with a clean tea cloth, and leave overnight in a cool place. The next day, rinse the vegetables well and turn them out onto a tea towel. Pat off any excess water.

Peel and grate the ginger and place in a small bowl with the flour, mustard powder, turmeric, nutmeg, and 2 tablespoons of the vinegar. Mix well to form a smooth paste. Set aside.

Place the vegetables in a preserving pan with the remaining vinegar and simmer, stirring carefully every now and then, until the vegetables are tender but not mushy, about 20 minutes. Add the sugar.

Temper the flour paste by adding about 2 tablespoons of the hot vinegar from the preserving pan and mixing well. Stir the tempered paste into the preserving pan with the vegetables. Simmer for 10 minutes until the cooking liquid is thick and glossy.

Ladle the piccalilli into the sterilized jars, seal with the lids, and store in a cool dark cupboard.

MAKES SIX 8-OZ JARS

romano bean chutney

One of my memories growing up is of eating runner beans from my dad's garden. My mum would make great chutney with them. Now that I have someone to grow things for me again I asked Nick, my husband, to plant runner beans. Unfortunately they are hard to find in America and do not do well in the warm Mediterranean Napa Valley climate. However, we did find that Italian Romano beans, which have much of the same flavor and texture, grow brilliantly here.

Preheat oven to 225ºF.

Sterilize six 8-oz jars and their lids by cleaning them upside down in the dishwasher using the sanitizing cycle. Place the washed jars in the oven for about 30 minutes.

Trim the beans and cut into 1-inch pieces. Bring a large pan of water to boil, add the beans, and cook until tender, 3–5 minutes. Drain and set side.

Finely chop the onions and add them to a large preserving pan along with 1 cup of the vinegar. Bring to a boil and simmer gently for 15 minutes. Add the reserved beans and all but 2 tablespoons of the vinegar. Cook for another 10 minutes, then add the sugar and simmer until it is dissolved. In a small bowl, mix together the remaining 2 tablespoons vinegar, cornstarch, turmeric, and English mustard powder to make a smooth paste. Add the paste to the simmering vegetables then bring back to a gentle boil until thickened, about 15 minutes.

Ladle the chutney into the sterilized jars, seal with the lids, and store in a cool dark cupboard.

MAKES SIX 8-OZ JARS

2 lbs. Romano beans
2 large onions
3 ½ cups white distilled vinegar
1 cup light brown sugar
1 tablespoon cornstarch
1 tablespoon turmeric
1 tablespoon English mustard powder

GILL'S NOTES

The acid and mustard in this chutney make it a great accompaniment to a grilled ham steak and a couple of poached free-range eggs for breakfast.

indian tomato chutney

When you think of the cuisine from Britain, you probably conjure up images of fish and chips or bangers and mash. Surprisingly, the most popular food in Britain is Indian. Go to the tiniest village and you will find a curry house. With this background, I learned a good deal about Indian cuisine and came up with this sweet and spicy chutney for when tomatoes are in abundance.

2 lbs. large ripe tomatoes
2-inch piece of ginger root
6 cloves garlic
¼ teaspoon crushed
   red pepper flakes
¼ teaspoon fennel seeds
¼ teaspoon fenugreek

¼ teaspoon nigella seeds
¼ teaspoon cumin seeds
¼ teaspoon black mustard seeds
2 tablespoons extra-virgin olive oil
⅔ cup fine sugar
2 teaspoons salt
6 dried apricots

Bring a large pot of water to a boil. Prepare a large bowl of ice water. Cut a small cross in the base of each tomato. Submerge the tomatoes in the boiling water for about 1 minute, or until the skin around the cut starts to curl. Remove immediately with a slotted spoon and place in the ice water to halt further cooking. When cool to the touch, slip off the loosened skins.

Core and roughly chop the tomatoes and place in a large bowl, pouring in any juice that collects on the cutting board. Grate the ginger and crush the garlic and place in a small bowl.

Place the red pepper flakes, fennel seeds, fenugreek, nigella seeds, cumin seeds, and black mustard seeds in a small bowl. Heat the olive oil in a large shallow sauté pan and add the spices and fry for a few seconds until the mustard seeds pop. Add the garlic and ginger and fry for another 20 seconds, being careful not to burn the garlic. Add the chopped tomatoes, sugar, and salt. Cover with a lid and continue to cook on low-medium heat for 45 minutes. Finely chop the dried apricots, add to the tomato mixture, and continue to cook for another 15 minutes.

Cool and serve with a quiche or frittata for breakfast, or warm naan bread as an appetizer.

SERVES 4-6

INN FOOD

mulled cranberry relish

2 ½ cups sugar

¼ cup port

½ cup red wine vinegar

¼ cup apple cider vinegar

8 cups cranberries

¾ teaspoon ground coriander

1 stick cinnamon

Zest and juice of 1 orange

GILL'S NOTES

You can use frozen cranberries if making this out of season. This relish is great with hot or cold turkey for Thanksgiving.

In England, we frequently serve fruit chutneys with hot or cold meats. That particular tradition only seems to appear in America with cranberry sauce and turkey. Sweet and savory flavor combinations, however, often turn up for breakfast. I created this rich relish to accompany breakfast sausages.

Preheat oven to 225°F.

Sterilize five 8-oz jars and their lids by cleaning them upside down in the dishwasher using the sanitizing cycle. Place the washed jars in the oven for about 30 minutes.

In a large saucepan over medium heat, gently cook the sugar, port, red wine vinegar, and apple cider vinegar until the sugar is dissolved. Add the cranberries, coriander, cinnamon stick, and orange juice and zest and bring to a slow boil. Simmer for about an hour, stirring occasionally but being careful not to break up the cranberries.

Ladle the relish into the sterilized jars, seal with the lids, and store in a cool dark cupboard. The relish is best left for a few weeks before using.

MAKES FIVE 8-OZ JARS

harvest cake

Think of Napa Valley and you think of wine. We started making our own wine soon after we arrived here, when our great friends and chosen family Simon and Avia moved to town and their lovely Homage Vineyard. We even planted a few rows of our very own Pinot Gris at the front of the Craftsman Inn. Now, whether the grapes are from the impeccably tended Homage Vineyard or our own more humble plot, we look forward all year to harvest as the pinnacle of the season.

After a long day of picking, crushing, and starting the grapes on their journey to become wine, we always celebrate with a grand harvest party to give thanks to all who have helped bring in the bounty. I created this harvest cake as a special contribution to the festivities. On harvest day, I use the same grapes we have picked for the wine: sweet, complex, and perfectly complemented by the rich olive oil and the bittersweet orange.

Sitting next to the vineyard under a harvest moon, sipping a glass of wine that was created here, and enjoying this perfect cake—for me, this captures the essence of Napa Valley life.

Preheat oven to 350°F.

Prepare a 9-inch springform cake pan by lightly brushing the bottom with olive oil and sprinkling with flour. Bring the butter to room temperature.

In the bowl of a stand mixer fitted with the flat paddle attachment, cream together the butter, sugar, orange zest, and bitters until well combined, about 1 minute.

In a separate bowl, mix together the eggs, olive oil, and sweet sherry then add to the mixer scraping down the sides of the bowl before mixing. Carefully mix in the flour to form a smooth batter. Pour into the prepared cake pan.

Scatter the grapes over the top and sprinkle with the raw cane sugar.

Bake for 45 minutes then cool on a wire rack. Allow to cool completely, preferably overnight. This cake is delicious served with my homemade vanilla yogurt (see recipe page 121) or crème fraiche.

SERVES 10–12

¾ cup extra-virgin olive oil

1 ¼ cups self-rising flour*

½ cup unsalted butter

¾ cup soft brown sugar

Zest of 1 orange

3 drops orange bitters

3 large eggs

¼ cup sweet sherry

¾ cup ripe red grapes

2 tablespoons raw cane sugar

GILL'S NOTES

Try to get ripe, sweet grapes. The cooking concentrates the flavor so even supermarket grapes will still taste good. If using wine grapes, carefully cut them nearly in half, open them up like a book. Remove the seeds, then close the grapes up, place them on to the top of the batter. With seedless grapes follow the recipe as written.

* If you cannot find self-rising flour, use 1 ¼ cups all-purpose flour mixed with 1 ¼ teaspoons baking powder and ¼ teaspoon salt as a substitute.

apple and cherry galette

4 large apples

4 tablespoons butter

⅔ cup sugar

½ quantity of semolina pastry
   (see recipe page 118)

¼ cup dried cherries

Zest of 1 orange

GILL'S NOTES

The secret to this recipe is my semolina pastry. It provides just the right balance of sweetness, absorbency, and crispness to yield perfect results. The folding and turning of the pastry is hard to describe, but take a look at the picture and you will see what the finished pie should resemble.

You can substitute pears and dried sweetened cranberries for the apples and dried cherries. Crème fraiche, vanilla ice cream, or custard all make great accompaniments.

I love recipes that are easy to prepare but produce gorgeous results. This free-form pie couldn't be simpler, but the rustic look and lovely aromas are sure to impress.

Preheat oven to 375ºF.

Line a large baking sheet with parchment paper. Core, peel, and slice the apples into wedges. In a sauté pan over medium heat, warm 3 tablespoons of the butter. When the froth subsides, add the apple wedges. Cook for about 5 minutes, until the apple edges just start to color. Add the sugar and continue to cook a few more minutes, or until the sugar melts and becomes a light caramel that coats the apples. Set aside.

Roll the pastry out into a 12-inch circle and place on the prepared baking sheet. Mix the dried cherries and orange zest into the cooled apple mixture. Spoon the filling into the middle of the pastry circle, spreading it out to cover the center and leaving about 3 inches uncovered all around. Lift up an edge of the pastry and fold over at an angle. Make another fold of the same size that just overlaps the previous fold. Continue around the full pastry circle, folding and overlapping in the same direction until the filling is surrounded by a nice border. Dot the filling with the remaining 1 tablespoon butter and bake until the pastry is golden brown, about 25 minutes. Serve warm or cold.

SERVES 6

spiced apple cider

If you are American and visit the West Country of England, where I come from, be very careful if you go into the local pub and order a pint of cider, which the locals call scrumpy. Instead of the refreshing, freshly squeezed apple juice you were expecting, you will receive 20 ounces of flat, dry fermented juice with an alcohol content closer to wine than beer. Drink two or three pints and you will need to be carried home!

Shortly after we moved to Napa Valley, we discovered that some friends and winemakers had purchased a property with an untended heirloom cider apple orchard. The eventual plan was to plough it and make a vineyard, but meanwhile they were happy for us to pick the apples to make our own hard cider.

The recipe begins with non-alcoholic apple cider but then picks up a kick from the added spirits, so don't drink three pints of this either!

Stick the whole cloves into the skin of the orange, scattering evenly around the orange. Cut the peel from the lemon. Then, using a sharp knife, cut away only the yellow peel, which contains the zest, leaving behind the pith. (The remaining lemon flesh can be reserved for another use.) Place the clove-studded orange, lemon peel, cinnamon stick, and star anise in a large pot. Add the apple cider, bring to a slow boil, and simmer very gently for about 30 minutes to infuse the spices. Add the brandy and stir to combine. Serve warm.

SERVES 8

12 whole cloves
1 medium orange
1 medium lemon
1 stick cinnamon
4 star anise
8 cups apple cider
1 cup brandy

GILL'S NOTES

As an alternative, try substituting dark rum for the brandy. For a non-alcoholic version, leave out the spirits.

winter

bread and butter pudding

One of the unexpected delights of coming to America was discovering the pleasure of mixing sweet and savory things together for breakfast. If you had told me when I was young that I was going to eat sausages with thick pancakes and syrup, I would have said you were barking mad.

But it works. Like so many great things in America, the unexpected contrast and unusual combination can be brilliant. Having discovered this delight, I decided to pair this classic British dessert, or pudding as we call it, with crispy maple bacon. Trying to explain it to guests, my husband Nick refers to it as French toast on steroids; once they have tried it, they generally agree.

Carefully split the vanilla bean. In a medium saucepan over medium-high heat, combine the vanilla bean, cream, milk, and salt and bring to a boil. Take off the heat and let sit for 1 hour to allow the flavors to infuse.

Place the golden raisins and sherry in a small saucepan and just cover with water. Bring to a boil and simmer gently until the raisins are plumped and have absorbed all the liquid. Set aside to cool. Bring the butter to room temperature.

Preheat oven to 350°F.

Lightly grease a large baking dish. Generously butter each slice of Challah and cut it in half. Lay the halves, overlapping the edges, in the prepared dish.

In a large bowl, whisk together the eggs and sugar. Remove the vanilla bean from the cooled cream mixture then slowly pour the liquid into the egg mixture and whisk to combine.

Scatter the plumped raisins over and around the bread slices. Pour the custard mixture slowly over the slices making sure to soak them thoroughly.

Place the dish in a bain marie (a larger pan filled with boiling water) in the oven and bake until the custard is set and the bread is a golden brown, about 45 minutes.

Warm the honey in a small saucepan until it thins. Brush the warmed honey over the top of the cooked pudding, then sprinkle with confectioners' sugar. Serve immediately.

SERVES 6

---

1 vanilla bean
1 cup heavy whipping cream
1 cup milk
Pinch of salt
2 tablespoons golden raisins
¼ cup cream sherry
4 tablespoons unsalted butter
8 slices Challah bread
3 eggs
½ cup sugar
1 tablespoon honey
Confectioners' sugar

GILL'S NOTES

Challah, a traditional Jewish egg bread, is my favorite for this recipe. French bread, brioche, or even panettone also work well and give subtle variations to the recipe. If using panettone, you can leave out the golden raisins. The honey can be replaced with marmalade or a peach preserve. This dish also makes a delicious dessert.

breakfast ravioli

4 oz. thinly sliced prosciutto

1 cup homemade ricotta (see recipe
    page 120)

1 cup grated parmesan cheese,
    plus 1 tablespoon

Salt and freshly ground black pepper

12 large egg yolks

12 oz. fresh homemade or
    store-bought pasta sheets

1 medium shallot, finely chopped

1 tablespoon extra-virgin olive oil

1 tablespoon butter

1 lb. baby spinach

GILL'S NOTES

*When you close up the ravioli, try to
expel as much air as possible without
breaking the delicate egg yolk.*

*Use the best eggs you can find for this
recipe and you will be rewarded when
the warm yolk creates a delicious sauce
right before your eyes when you cut
into the tender parcels.*

*Store-bought ricotta is a fine alternative
if you don't want to make your own.*

My friend Avia keeps her own chickens and is kind enough to share some of her "girls'" eggs with me. The yolks of these beautiful free-range eggs are so firm, golden, and delicious that I just had to find something special to do with them. Bacon and eggs provided inspiration. The cooked prosciutto is like bacon's evil twin, tantalizing morsels of porky goodness that are perfect with the wonderful yolks.

In a skillet over medium heat, gently cook the prosciutto slices until the fat renders and the bottom of the slices turns a light golden brown. Flip the slices and cook for a few seconds more. Transfer to a paper towel to drain the excess fat and cool.

In a bowl, mix together the ricotta and 1 cup of the grated parmesan. When well combined, crumble the cooked prosciutto into the cheese mixture and distribute evenly. Season with pepper only (the prosciutto will add sufficient salt). Lay out the rolled pasta sheets and cut each into 12 4-by-8-inch rectangles. Place 2 tablespoons of the cheese and prosciutto filling in the middle of one side of the rectangle. Using your thumb or the back of a spoon, make an indentation in the top of the filling. Carefully place an egg yolk into the indentation. Brush the edges of the rectangle with water then gently fold the uncovered half over the filling and press the edges together to seal the ravioli.

In a large skillet over medium heat, warm the olive oil and butter. Add the chopped shallot and cook until translucent, about 3 minutes. Add the baby spinach, gently mix and season, cover, and cook until just wilted, 1–2 minutes. Cover to keep warm.

Bring 4 quarts of salted water to a boil in a large pot. Using a slotted spoon, gently place some ravioli in the water (cook in batches as needed). Gently boil until the pasta is cooked through but the egg yolks are still runny, about 4 minutes To serve, place some cooked spinach in the center of a warm plate. Top with 1 or 2 ravioli. Add a sprinkle of parmesan and serve immediately. You can serve this dish as 12 smaller portions, as part of a multi-course breakfast or brunch, or 6 larger portions.

SERVES 6-12.

chocolate chip banana bread

My mother-in-law was 10, and her younger brother was just a toddler, when the Second World War broke out. After the war, she remembers seeing the first bananas back in the shops, and her little brother having no idea what they were; she bought him one, and he started to eat it without removing the peel. Now we take the availability of bananas year-round for granted and are used to eating this tropical fruit even during winter. I love to make this recipe for banana bread with chocolate chips as the flavors complement each other well.

Preheat oven to 350°F.

Grease and line a 9-by-5-inch loaf pan with parchment paper.

Bring the butter to room temperature. In the bowl of a stand mixer fitted with the paddle attachment, blend the butter and vanilla sugar for 3 minutes on high speed until the mixture is pale yellow.

In a medium bowl, mash the bananas with a fork. Mix in the eggs and almond extract then add to the butter mixture. Scrape down the sides of the bowl and blend for another minute.

In a small bowl, combine the flour and ground almonds, then add to the mixer bowl. Blend on low speed until the batter is smooth. Scrape down the sides of the bowl and add the chocolate chips, dried cranberries, and slivered almonds, and blend to combine.

Spoon the batter into the prepared loaf pan, smoothing the top with a spatula.

Bake for 70–80 minutes, until a toothpick inserted in the center of the bread comes out clean.

Cool in the loaf pan for 20 minutes on a wire rack before turning out onto a board. Let the bread cool completely before slicing.

MAKES ONE 9-BY-5-INCH LOAF (10–12 SLICES)

½ cup unsalted butter
¾ cup vanilla sugar (see note)
3 medium ripe bananas
2 eggs
¼ teaspoon almond extract
1½ cups self-rising flour*
¼ cup ground almonds
1 cup semi-sweet chocolate chips
1 cup dried cranberries
½ cup slivered almonds

GILL'S NOTES

Vanilla sugar is easy to make: slice the side of a whole vanilla bean, scrape out the sides, and bury in 2 cups of sugar for a week or so, allowing the vanilla to permeate the sugar.

For a Christmas treat, you can substitute white chocolate chips.

* If you cannot find self-rising flour, use 1½ cups all-purpose flour mixed with 1½ teaspoons baking powder and ½ teaspoon salt as a substitute.

the best shortbread

1 cup unsalted butter
½ cup sugar
⅔ cup semolina flour
1 cup all-purpose flour

GILL'S NOTES

Enjoy this shortbread with your breakfast or afternoon cup of tea. It also makes a great accompaniment to a rich creamy dessert, such as lemon posset or panna cotta (see recipe page 121).

For a variation kids will love, add ½ cup chocolate chips to the dough.

If you have ever visited Scotland, you will know that it is the spiritual home of shortbread. Petticoat tails in tartan tins are everywhere, making a quick treat if you do not have time to make your own. My version is light and crumbly, with just a little crunch from the semolina flour. I think you will agree that, despite my not being a Scot, it's the best shortbread ever!

Preheat oven to 300ºF.

Line 2 large baking sheets with parchment paper.

Bring the butter to room temperature. In the bowl of a stand mixer fitted with the paddle attachment, cream the butter and sugar until pale yellow. Add the semolina and all-purpose flour and mix until the dough comes away from the sides of the bowl.

Turn the dough out onto a lightly floured surface and cut into 2 pieces. Roll out each piece to a thickness of ¼ inch. Cut into rounds using a 2½-inch cookie cutter. Place 1 inch apart on the prepared baking sheets. Bake for 35 minutes. Cool on wire racks.

MAKES 30 COOKIES

granny frowan's welsh cakes

Granny Frowan was my great grandmother. She grew up in a Welsh coal mining village with the tongue twisting name of Ynysybwl (roughly pronounced "Un-iss-u-bull" in English). Her husband toiled in the pit on which the village depended and, like so many others, succumbed to silicosis at the age of only 57. That was 1937 and granny Frowan went to live with her daughter, my grandmother, in Bristol. She brought with her a giant piece of heavy steel called a Welsh bake stone that she had used over the open coal fire at home. My mum was fascinated by the ritual of slow heating the stone to make these traditional cakes. I don't really remember granny Frowan, but I remember vividly my mum working away making Welsh Cakes, which she does to this day. She uses a griddle, as I do here, rather than the traditional bake stone. Mum always has a sparkle in her eye and a softness in her voice when making these cakes and remembering Granny Frowan.

Sift the flour into a large bowl. Cut the cold butter into small cubes then rub into the flour using your fingers until the mixture resembles fine breadcrumbs. Add the sugar, raisins, and salt and gently mix.

In a small bowl, whisk together the eggs and the milk, then combine with the dry ingredients to form a soft dough.

Turn out the dough onto a lightly floured work surface and roll it out to a ½-inch thickness. Cut into 3-inch rounds with a plain cutter.

Heat an ungreased griddle pan over low heat. Place the cakes on the griddle pan and cook for 6–7 minutes on each side until they turn a golden brown color.

Let cool then cut the cakes in half crosswise to form 2 disks. Serve with butter.

MAKES 20 CAKES

2 ½ cups self-rising flour*
1 cup cold unsalted butter
¾ cup granulated sugar
1 cup small raisins
¼ teaspoon salt
3 large eggs
2 tablespoons whole milk

GILL'S NOTES

Use the heaviest griddle you can find for these cakes. You can even buy a traditional Welsh bake stone from Wales if you want to be authentic. Whatever you use, heat it slowly and thoroughly. Watch the cakes carefully; there is a short cooking window between the desired golden brown and overdone dark brown. Always wipe your griddle clean between batches.

Currants can be substituted for the small raisins. Serve these cakes with butter for breakfast, or with honey butter or clotted cream and strawberry jam for an alternative to scones with afternoon tea.

* If you cannot find self-rising flour. use 2 ½ cups all-purpose flour mixed with 2 ½ teaspoons baking powder and ¾ teaspoon salt as a substitute.

portland cakes

¼ cup candied lemon peel

Zest from 1 lemon

2 tablespoons butter

1 cup dried blueberries

½ cup brown sugar

½ teaspoon mixed spice (see note)

Half quantity cream cheese pastry
   (see recipe page 118)

½ cup milk

2 tablespoons sugar

GILL'S NOTES

Mixed spice is a commonplace item in Britain that's readily available. In America, look for it in the international section of larger supermarkets or in a dedicated British Foods store. If you can't find it, blend your own by mixing together:

2 tablespoons ground cinnamon

2 teaspoons ground nutmeg

1 teaspoon ground ginger

½ teaspoon ground coriander

½ teaspoon ground cloves

Use what you need and store the rest in a small airtight container.

The phrase "selling like hot cakes" may have originated from the incredible popularity of two renowned British pastries, Eccles cakes and Banbury cakes. Both are similar, with spiced currants in a puff pastry crust, though inhabitants of either town would defend the uniqueness of their cake with vigor! Living in America, I found currants, which are actually dried Zante grapes originally from the Greek island of the same name, hard to come by. So instead of using currants, I started experimenting with something very American, the dried Blueberry, and produced these smashing little morsels to continue the hot cakes tradition. When it came to a name, I originally called them a rather wordy "blueberry cream cheese pastry." Searching for a more appropriate title associated with a place, I asked my friend Simon, the "rain man" of general knowledge, where blueberries are best. Portland, Oregon and Portland, Maine was his instant reply. So, here they are: Portland cakes.

Preheat oven to 400°F.

Line a large baking sheet with parchment paper. Finely chop the candied lemon peel. In a small saucepan over medium heat, melt the butter then let cool for a few minutes. In a bowl, mix together the dried blueberries, chopped candied lemon peel, zest, brown sugar, mixed spice, and melted butter and set aside.

Roll out the cream cheese pastry on a lightly floured work surface to a ⅛-inch thickness. Using a 4-inch circular cutter, cut the pastry into rounds.

Place 1 heaping teaspoon of the fruit filling in the middle of each pastry circle. Brush the edges of the pastry with water, fold them into the middle, and seal well. Turn the pastries over so the sealed edge is on the bottom. Gently flatten then slash three cuts on the top of each cake with a sharp knife.

Place the cakes on the prepared baking sheet. Brush with the milk and sprinkle with the sugar, then bake for 20 minutes. Serve warm or at room temperature.

MAKES 16 CAKES

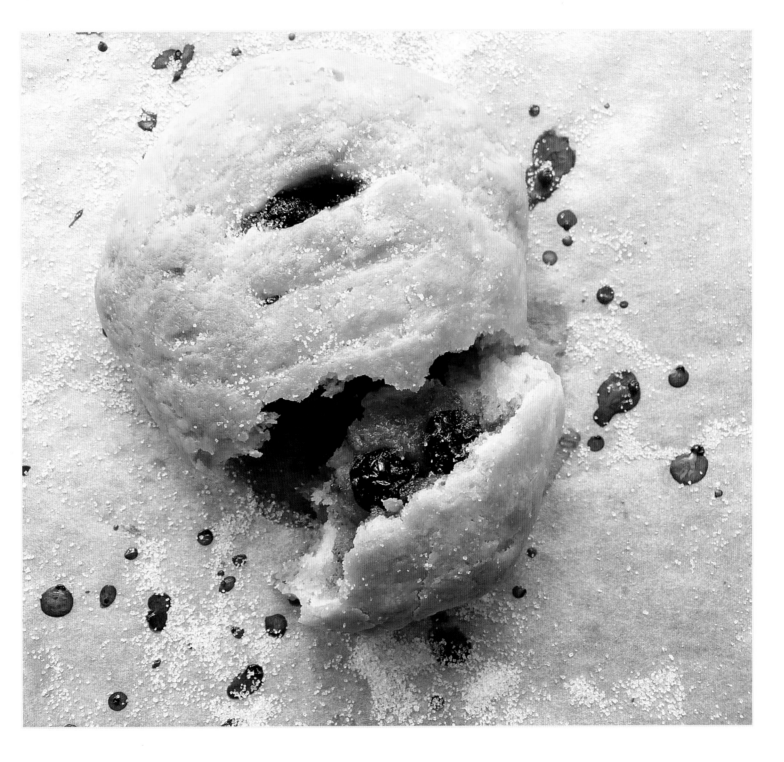

oatmeal and more cookies

I like classic American chocolate chip cookies. However, I often find the consistency either too crumbly and toffee-like or too crisp and dry. One of the best recipes I've found is from my friend Melanie, and it yields cookies that have great texture and are not oversweet. Building on her recipe, I tried lots of variations until I got it just right.

We serve these in our rooms with a decanter of sherry as a nightcap treat for our guests. When my husband Nick checks people in, he always tells them where the cookie jar is because he knows they are addictive. They have so much more to offer than just oatmeal. One bite, and you'll be hooked!

Preheat oven to 350°F.

Line a few large baking sheets with parchment paper.

Sift the flour, mixed spice, baking powder, and salt into a medium bowl. Bring the butter to room temperature. In the bowl of a stand mixer fitted with the flat paddle attachment, cream the butter and sugar on medium speed for 3 minutes. Add the beaten egg and vanilla extract, continue mixing until smooth, then scrape down the sides of the bowl. Turn the mixer speed to low then add the sifted dry ingredients. Add the walnuts, rolled oats, chocolate chips, and dried cherries and mix until just combined.

Drop heaping tablespoons of the dough onto the prepared baking sheets, spacing each mound 1 inch apart. Bake for 15 minutes. Cool on wire racks.

MAKES 20 COOKIES

1 cup all-purpose flour
½ teaspoon mixed spice (see recipe page 104)
½ teaspoon baking powder
¼ teaspoon salt
1 cup unsalted butter
1 cup brown sugar
1 egg, beaten
1 teaspoon pure vanilla extract
1 cup chopped walnuts
3 cups rolled oats
1 cup chocolate chips
½ cup dried cherries

GILL'S NOTES

It's important to form the cookies all the same size so that they cook evenly. Make a few thousand and you will soon find you can do that easily. A small ice cream scoop is a useful tool for ensuring consistent portions.

Don't try and rush the cooking: bake the cookies one baking sheet at a time, and in the center of your oven, so they cook evenly.

christmas scones

The red stripes of candy canes have long been used as a Christmas decoration. Here, I use them to decorate scones, giving this classic British treat both the traditional taste and look of the holiday season. When celebrating with our American friends, they were an instant hit. Now I make them for my guests throughout December. Everyone says these scones get them in the holiday spirit.

2 cups all-purpose flour	½ cup shelled pistachios
⅓ cup granulated sugar	½ cup dried cranberries
1 tablespoon baking powder	3 tablespoons butter
1 teaspoon cream of tartar	1 ½ cups heavy whipping cream
¼ teaspoon salt	½ teaspoon peppermint extract
½ cup rolled oats	¾ cup confectioners' sugar
1 cup white chocolate chips	3 peppermint candy canes

Preheat oven to 400°F.

Line a large baking sheet with parchment paper. Sift the flour, sugar, baking powder, cream of tartar, and salt into a large bowl. Add the rolled oats, chocolate chips, pistachios, and dried cranberries. In a small saucepan over medium heat, melt the butter then let cool for a few minutes. Reserve 1 tablespoon of the melted butter. In a small bowl, mix together the remaining 2 tablespoons butter with the cream and peppermint extract. Carefully combine the butter mixture with the dry ingredients, working gently with a spatula until the dough comes away from the sides of the bowl. Turn the dough out onto a lightly floured work surface and divide into 2 equal pieces. Form each piece into a 6-inch round then divide each round into 6 wedges. Place the 12 wedges onto the prepared baking sheet. Brush with the reserved tablespoon of butter and bake for 15–17 minutes.

Cool for a few minutes on a wire rack. To make the glaze, slowly add water to the confectioners' sugar, stirring, until it has a honey-like consistency. Drizzle sparingly over the warm scones. Place the peppermint candy canes in a small zip-top freezer bag, crush them with a rolling pin, and scatter the pieces on top of the glaze. Cool completely before serving.

MAKES 12 SCONES

spiced apples

5 medium apples

Zest and juice of 1 orange

¼ cup raw cane sugar

¼ cup cream sherry

1 cup Chardonnay

5 cloves

2 star anise

1 stick cinnamon

GILL'S NOTES

These spiced apples are great on their own. I also like to serve them on top of my homemade granola with a little homemade vanilla yogurt (see recipe page 121).

Between Napa Valley and the Pacific coast lies the farm country of Sonoma County. In many areas, where the climate and soil are just right, grapes are the main crop. Elsewhere, extensive apple orchards flourish. There are dozens of varieties, and the harvest usually starts off with the versatile Gravenstein and finishes with a winter variety like Fuji or Pink Lady. You can cook this dish throughout apple season, but I think winter is the perfect time to enjoy the mellow spices and rich apple flavors. I find it's just the thing to cheer me up on a foggy damp morning.

Preheat oven to 375°F.

Grease a 9-by-12-inch ovenproof baking dish.

Peel, core, and cut the apples into ½-inch slices. In a medium bowl, combine the slices with the orange zest and juice, making sure they are completely covered to prevent discoloration.

In a small saucepan over a low heat, heat the sugar, cream sherry, and Chardonnay until the sugar dissolves. Using a slotted spoon, transfer the apple slices to the prepared baking dish and discard the liquid. Pour the warm wine mixture over the slices and scatter the cloves, star anise, and cinnamon stick over the top.

Bake for 35–40 minutes, or until the apples are cooked but not mushy. Cool for 5 minutes. Remove the whole spices before serving.

SERVES 8

spiced raisin and almond granola

I make a few varieties of granola for the Inns. They proved so popular that I decided to sell them at the local farmers' market and in local stores. If you would like to get your own stash, find out how to order some on page 122. Those granolas are great throughout the year served with cold milk, homemade yogurt, and fruit, or just munched straight from the bag for a sustaining snack. This recipe is a winter version to be enjoyed with warm milk. The aroma of the mixed spice evokes memories of my mum's mince pies baking for Christmas.

Preheat oven to 315°F.

Line a large baking sheet with parchment paper.

In a small pan over medium heat, warm the honey and canola oil until evenly mixed. In a large mixing bowl, combine the oats, slivered almonds, flaxseeds, sunflower seeds, mixed spice, and orange zest. Add the warm honey mixture and combine well, making sure all the oats are covered. Turn out the granola onto the prepared baking sheet and spread out to an even thickness.

Bake for 30 minutes. Cool on a wire rack. Once completely cooled, break up the clumps of granola into a large mixing bowl and add the raisins. Store in an airtight container. Serve with warm milk.

SERVES 10

¼ cup honey
¼ cup canola oil
3 cups oats
¼ cup slivered almonds
¼ cup flax seeds
¼ cup sunflower seeds
1 teaspoon mixed spice
Zest of 1 orange
¼ cup raisins

GILL'S NOTES

If you can't find mixed spice in your local store, you can make your own (see recipe in note for Portland Cakes on page 104).

sparkling mimosa

Your favorite sparkling wine
2 cubes raw cane sugar
4 drops orange bitters
2 tablespoons Campari

GILL'S NOTES

You can find orange bitters in most specialty drink stores or better supermarkets. Don't skip them as the tangy orange taste really makes this drink special. That said, you can adjust the quantity of Campari and bitters for the sweet-bitter balance that suits your palate.

Chances are good you will spot a bottle of Campari in the background of any bar scene from a classic 1960s movie. When I recently saw a character on "Mad Men" sipping a campari, I just had to go out and buy a bottle. I was thrilled to rediscover it. Campari has since become my new favorite aperitif, replacing my usual glass of bubbly. Which got me to thinking—why not enjoy both my favorites? After a little experimentation, I came up with this simple and light drink, which you can enjoy as a start to the evening or, even better, with a late-morning brunch to get your weekend off to a good start.

Chill two champagne glasses. You can use flutes as we tend to nowadays, or dig out the 1960s bowl-style glasses from the back of the cupboard for a genuine "Mad Men" feel. Place a cube of sugar in each glass and shake in a few drops of orange bitters. Cover the sugar cube with the Campari then top off with your favorite sparkling wine.

SERVES 2

additional recipes

This refreshing salad and the bright pico de gallo salsa are colorful and different dishes to serve for breakfast, brunch, or a light lunch alongside any rich and cheesy plate, from deep-dish quiche to frittata or even a simple cheese omelet. If you grow your own tomatoes use those; if not, try to find one of the flavorful heirloom varieties from your local farmers' market or grocery store.

tomato, watermelon, and arugula salad

2 tablespoons extra-virgin olive oil

1 teaspoon white balsamic vinegar

**Sea salt and freshly ground
    white pepper**

1 lb. heirloom tomatoes

1 small seedless watermelon

8 oz. arugula

**1 small handful large leaf
    Italian basil**

This mix of ingredients really captures the flavors of summer. The acid of the tomatoes, sweetness of the watermelon, and slightly bitter arugula complement each other beautifully when combined with the basil and dressing. This is a perfect accompaniment for any egg and cheese dish or simply served on its own.

In a large bowl, whisk together the olive oil, vinegar, salt, and pepper. Slice the tomatoes. Peel and chop the watermelon into 1-inch cubes. Add the tomato slices and watermelon cubes to the dressing and carefully turn over until evenly coated. Arrange the arugula on a serving platter. Place the dressed tomatoes and watermelon over the top. Finely chop the basil and scatter it over the salad. Serve immediately.

SERVES 6

pico de gallo

1 lb. heirloom tomatoes

1 medium shallot

1 clove garlic

1 small jalapeño pepper

½ small bunch fresh cilantro

**Sea salt and freshly ground
    white pepper**

Juice of 1 lime

We have lots of Mexican Americans in our town, and we are lucky enough to be very close to a great little Mexican market. They make their own cooked salsa that my husband Nick loves but are too spicy for me. If your tastes are more like Nick's, you can turn the heat up in this recipe by using a serrano or even a habañero pepper instead of the jalapeño.

Place a colander in a large bowl. Chop the tomatoes into large dice. Finely chop the shallot, garlic, jalapeno, and cilantro. Place all of the chopped ingredients in the colander, season generously with salt and pepper, and leave for a few minutes. Turn the drained ingredients into a medium bowl, add the lime juice, and toss once. Adjust the seasoning and serve immediately.

SERVES 6

pastry recipes

Store-bought pastry, whether short crust or puff, is a great standby. But it really is easy to make your own. Master these few basic recipes, and you will have almost everything you'll ever need for any kind of sweet or savory baking project.

mum's savory pastry

½ **cup unsalted butter**

½ **cup lard**

2 **cups self-rising flour***

½ **teaspoon salt**

1 **large egg**

GILL'S NOTES

* If you cannot find self-rising flour, use 1 cup all-purpose flour mixed with 1 teaspoon baking powder and ¼ teaspoon salt as a substitue.

My mum has been making this pastry for years. She is so familiar with it that she doesn't even need to measure out the ingredients. Once you have tried this for your savory pies, I am sure you will make it so often it will become second nature to you, too.

In the bowl of a stand mixer fitted with the flat paddle attachment, cream the butter and lard. Sift in the flour, salt, and mix until the mixture resembles breadcrumbs. Whisk the egg then add to the flour mixture with just enough water to bring the mix together into a dough. Form into a ball then wrap in plastic wrap. Refrigerate for 1–2 hours before use.

MAKES TWO 9-INCH PIE CRUSTS

cream cheese pastry

1 **cup unsalted butter**

1 **cup cream cheese**

2 **tablespoon confectioners' sugar**

2 **cups self-rising flour***

1 **teaspoon salt**

*See note above

This pastry has a creamy edge to it and is a good alternative to puff pastry. It is also much easier to make.

In the bowl of a stand mixer fitted with the flat paddle attachment, cream the butter, cream cheese, and confectioners' sugar. Sift in the flour and salt and continue to mix on low to medium speed until the dough forms a ball. Wrap in plastic wrap and refrigerate for 1–2 hours before use.

MAKES TWO 12-INCH PIE CRUSTS

semolina pastry

½ cup semolina flour

1 ¾ cups all-purpose Flour

½ teaspoon salt

2 tablespoons sugar

1 cup cold unsalted butter

⅓ cup ice water

5 tablespoons plain yogurt

I love this type of pastry for pies and galettes. With a crisp crust, it suits soft fruits especially well as it soaks up the juices.

In the bowl of a stand mixer fitted with the paddle attachment, mix the semolina flour, all-purpose flour, salt, and sugar on low speed for 10 seconds. Cut the cold butter into small cubes. Add to the bowl and blend until the mixture has the consistency of coarse sand. Add the ice water and yogurt and mix until a smooth dough forms. Refrigerate the dough for about 30 minutes before use.

MAKES TWO 9-INCH PIE CRUSTS

sweet short crust pastry

1 cup unsalted butter

1½ cups confectioners' sugar

¼ teaspoon salt

2¾ cups all-purpose flour

4 egg yolks

2 tablespoons half-and-half

GILL'S NOTES

All-purpose flour is fine for most baking needs. If you are making something very delicate, and want a particularly light pastry, you can substitute an equal quantity of Italian "OO" flour. This is flour that has been very finely ground, giving pastry an airy texture. Pastry is easier to handle when chilled, and it freezes very well. If using frozen pastry, transfer it to the refrigerator the night before.

This pastry is great to use for open-faced tarts, like chocolate or lemon tarts. It has a taste that resembles shortbread.

In the bowl of a stand mixer fitted with the flat paddle attachment, cream the butter, sugar, and salt. Sift in the flour and mix. In a small bowl, whisk together the egg yolks and the half-and-half then add to the flour mixture. Mix on low to medium speed until the dough comes together. Form into a ball then wrap in plastic wrap. Refrigerate for 1–2 hours before use.

MAKES TWO 12-INCH PIE CRUSTS

dairy recipes

Look in your refrigerator and I am sure you will have a carton of cream and a jug of milk; they are staples that almost every household keeps. What you may not realize is just how much more you can do with basic dairy products. Master these simple recipes and it will be just like having your own creamery.

ricotta cheese

1 teaspoon citric acid
1 gallon whole milk
2 teaspoons salt

GILL'S NOTES

Add a spoonful of ricotta to your favorite pasta sauce for a rich and creamy finish.

If you have ever thought about making your own cheese, this is a great way to start and gives instant gratification with no need for brining, aging, or many of the other steps that other cheeses require. I love to make this simple ricotta because I can use whole (full-fat) milk and control the size of the curds to give a lovely, creamy texture that goes really well with fresh or cooked fruit.

Dissolve the citric acid in 2 fluid ouncles of water. Pour the milk into a large saucepan and add the citric acid solution and the salt. Place an accurate thermometer into the milk. Heat gently, stirring occasionally. As the milk warms, it will separate into curds and whey. Monitor the temperature closely until it reaches 185ºF.

Turn off the heat and allow the curds and whey to sit for about 10 minutes. Line a sieve with cheesecloth and strain the cheese through it; most of the whey will come through quite quickly but the cheese should be left to drain for at least an hour. Discard the whey. Form the ricotta into a ball, wrap in cheesecloth, and refrigerate until use.

MAKES APPROXIMATELY 3 CUPS

lemon posset

2 lemons
2½ cups heavy whipping cream
¾ cup sugar

GILL'S NOTES

You can substitute Meyer lemons or limes for interesting variations. This is great served with my shortbreads (see recipe page 100), or topped with finely crumbled Amaretti biscuits.

A posset is an old English milk drink that was curdled with wine or ale before citrus was readily available. This adaptation uses cream and lemons and makes a great dessert. This is such a simple dish to make but the result is surprisingly sophisticated with a great balance of sharp, sweet, and creamy flavors.

Zest one lemon. In a small bowl, combine the zest and the juice from both lemons. In a heavy-bottomed pot over medium heat, bring the cream and sugar to a gentle boil and simmer for 3 minutes. Remove from the heat and add the lemon juice and zest, whisking lightly.

Pour into 6 individual dishes, cover, and refrigerate until set, about 2–3 hours.

SERVES 6

vanilla yogurt

1 vanilla pod
4 cups whole milk
1 cup live yogurt
Home yogurt maker

GILL'S NOTES

You can use a cup from your previous batch of yogurt to start the next one. However, if you repeat that more than a few times the flavor will become too sour and you won't get as good a set. Restart with fresh live yogurt every third batch.

You can buy yogurt in a bewildering variety of flavors. Making your own is simple if you buy the right gadget; and once you have it, you'll never look back. I like the flavor of vanilla but you can omit it for traditional plain yogurt. You can also add a little cooked fruit to the bottom of the jars to create your own different varieties. Whichever flavor you produce, mix it with your granola for a wonderful start to your breakfast.

Slit the vanilla pod and squeeze to expose the seeds; place in a heavy-bottomed saucepan and add the milk. Over medium-high heat, warm to just below boiling point. Remove from the heat and cool immediately in an ice water bath. When the mixture is completely cool add the live yogurt and whisk lightly to incorporate. Strain into a jug and fill the jars of your yogurt maker. Run a 10-hour yogurt making cycle. Remove from the yogurt maker and refrigerate before serving.

MAKES 5 CUPS YOGURT

how to buy
Inn Food

My guests loved my granola so much that my husband Nick convinced me to package it for sale. It has been interesting learning all about the regulations, nutritional values, and other requirements needed to offer it for sale commercially. It took me a while to get everything sorted out, and now I have guests who buy bags direct, locals who get their granola fix at the farmers' market, and a few stores that stock it—as well as some other inns that buy it in bulk to serve to their guests.

If you would like to buy some, you can check current prices and order online at my website:

www.Inn-Food.com

Or you can always just drop me an e-mail at:

InnFood@TheCraftsmanInn.com

I hope you enjoy the granola and, for those who have stayed with me, that it brings back happy memories of breakfast at the inn.

recipe index

Here we list recipes in alphabetical order. The recipes are listed seasonally on the contents page.

A NOTE ON MEASUREMENTS

OVEN TEMPERATURES		DRY MEASURES			LIQUID MEASURES			
500°F : 240°C	2 cups	16 oz	450 g	4 cups	1 quart	32 fl oz	950 ml
400°F : 200°C	1 cup	8 oz	225 g	2 cups	1 pint	16 fl oz	480 ml
350°F : 180°C	³/₄ cup	6 oz	375 g	1 cups	½ pint	8 fl oz	240 ml
300°F : 150°C	½ cup	4 oz	115 g	½ cup	¼ pint	4 fl oz	150 ml
250°F : 120°C	¼ cup	2 oz	60 g	¼ cup	⅛ pint	2 fl oz	60 ml
	1 tablespoon	½ oz	15 g			1 fl oz	30 ml

index

DEDICATION

For my amazing children, Katie, Max, and Olivia I am so proud of all of you.

AUTHOR'S ACKNOWLEDGMENTS

I am grateful for the love, support and encouragement given to me by my wonderful children, my friends, and family. Great thanks to Jeff and Sally Manfredi for letting me use even more of their lovely pottery than I already own and for being my official taste testers of record for my new recipes. Thanks also to Simon and Avia Hawksworth for sharing the bounty of their beautiful Homage Vineyard, as well as their love and friendship, so generously.

Thank you to my wonderful husband, Nick, for his continued love and patience; without him this book would never have happened. I have known Nick since adolescence; we have learned about life together as we have traveled the world and raised three wonderful children: Katie, so in love with the Napa Valley that she chose a wine country wedding to seal the knot with the love of her life, Ryan; Max, following in my footsteps at culinary school and cooking in our favorite local restaurant, Jole; and Olivia, a force of nature whose determination shows up strongly in the kitchen as she perseveres to make what she wants to make, as good as she wants it to be.

And finally, a special thank you to my collaborator, and now really good friend, Gaye Allen. Gaye's brilliant creative, photographic, and publishing skills have made this book something I am truly proud of.

PUBLISHER'S ACKNOWLEDGMENTS

I am so grateful to have been introduced to Gillian Kite by my good friend and neighbor Kathy Foster, who has the extraordinarily generous skill of connecting like-minded souls, in particular those with a shared love of food and wine. How right she was! In the Kites I was so happy to discover, not only fellow Brits, but fellow Bristolians, similarly transplanted to this amazing, bounteous, place. After almost 30 years of making books, including literally hundreds of cookbooks on both sides of "the pond," making this one in the warmth of Gillian's Calistoga kitchen, has been a uniquely fun and enjoyable experience.

Gill's guests simply *love* her food, and having been an unofficial taster making this book, I can see why. I am also very grateful to Nick Kite, for his most generous hospitality, and for being our "official translator," without whom this book may best have been enjoyed in Bristol!

I would like to thank talented photographer, Bruce Fleming, for permission to use the wonderful landscapes that introduce each season. No one captures the beauty of the Napa Valley better in any season. Thank you also, to the insightful publisher Hannah Rahill, for some very sound, early editorial guidance and to Polly Nyberg and Judy Cortesi for the loan of lovely props.

I'd also be remiss not to thank *my* wonderful parents for the prophetic decision to raise their family in Bristol! Bristol and Liverpool: the two gateway ports to America. From Liverpool, you got the Beatles; from Bristol, you got? Cabot, Brunel, oh... and this cookbook!